Season: _____

Date: _____

Location: _____

Weather/Elements

_____
_____
_____
_____

Place/Location/Habitat

_____
_____
_____
_____

Sights/Sounds & Activity

_____
_____
_____

Bird Species/Markings/Features

_____
_____
_____

Notes

Season: _____

Date: _____ Time: _____

Location: _____

Weather/Elements
_____
_____
_____
_____

Place/Location/Habitat
_____
_____
_____
_____

Sights/Sounds & Activity
_____
_____
_____

Bird Species/Markings/Features
_____
_____
_____

Notes

Season: _____

Date: _____ Time: _____

Location: _____

Weather/Elements
_____
_____
_____
_____

Place/Location/Habitat
_____
_____
_____
_____

Sights/Sounds & Activity
_____
_____
_____

Bird Species/Markings/Features
_____
_____
_____

Notes

Season: _____

Date: _____ Time: _____

Location: _____

Weather/Elements
_____
_____
_____
_____

Place/Location/Habitat
_____
_____
_____
_____

Sights/Sounds & Activity
_____
_____
_____

Bird Species/Markings/Features
_____
_____
_____

Notes

Season: _____

Date: _____ Time: _____

Location: _____

Weather/Elements
_____
_____
_____
_____

Place/Location/Habitat
_____
_____
_____
_____

Sights/Sounds & Activity
_____
_____
_____

Bird Species/Markings/Features
_____
_____
_____

Notes

Season: _____

Date: _____ Time: _____

Location: _____

Weather/Elements
_____
_____
_____
_____

Place/Location/Habitat
_____
_____
_____
_____

Sights/Sounds & Activity
_____
_____
_____

Bird Species/Markings/Features
_____
_____
_____

Notes

Season: _____

Date: _____ Time: _____

Location: _____

Weather/Elements
_____
_____
_____
_____

Place/Location/Habitat
_____
_____
_____
_____

Sights/Sounds & Activity
_____
_____
_____

Bird Species/Markings/Features
_____
_____
_____

Notes

Season: _____

Date: _____ Time: _____

Location: _____

Weather/Elements
_____
_____
_____
_____

Place/Location/Habitat
_____
_____
_____
_____

Sights/Sounds & Activity
_____
_____
_____

Bird Species/Markings/Features
_____
_____
_____

Notes

Season: _____

Date: _____ Time: _____

Location: _____

Weather/Elements
_____
_____
_____
_____

Place/Location/Habitat
_____
_____
_____
_____

Sights/Sounds & Activity
_____
_____
_____

Bird Species/Markings/Features
_____
_____
_____

Notes

Season: _____

Date: _____ Time: _____

Location: _____

Weather/Elements
_____
_____
_____
_____

Place/Location/Habitat
_____
_____
_____
_____

Sights/Sounds & Activity
_____
_____
_____

Bird Species/Markings/Features
_____
_____
_____

Notes

Season: _____

Date: _____ Time: _____

Location: _____

Weather/Elements
_____
_____
_____
_____

Place/Location/Habitat
_____
_____
_____
_____

Sights/Sounds & Activity
_____
_____
_____

Bird Species/Markings/Features
_____
_____
_____

Notes

Season: _____

Date: _____ Time: _____

Location: _____

Weather/Elements

_____
_____
_____
_____

Place/Location/Habitat

_____
_____
_____
_____

Sights/Sounds & Activity

_____
_____
_____

Bird Species/Markings/Features

_____
_____
_____

Notes

Season: _____

Date: _____ Time: _____

Location: _____

Weather/Elements
_____
_____
_____
_____

Place/Location/Habitat
_____
_____
_____
_____

Sights/Sounds & Activity
_____
_____
_____

Bird Species/Markings/Features
_____
_____
_____

Notes

Season: _____

Date: _____ Time: _____

Location: _____

Weather/Elements

_____
_____
_____
_____

Place/Location/Habitat

_____
_____
_____
_____

Sights/Sounds & Activity

_____
_____
_____

Bird Species/Markings/Features

_____
_____
_____

Notes

Season: _____

Date: _____ Time: _____

Location: _____

Weather/Elements

_____
_____
_____
_____

Place/Location/Habitat

_____
_____
_____
_____

Sights/Sounds & Activity

_____
_____
_____

Bird Species/Markings/Features

_____
_____
_____

Notes

Season: _____

Date: _____ Time: _____

Location: _____

Weather/Elements
_____
_____
_____
_____

Place/Location/Habitat
_____
_____
_____
_____

Sights/Sounds & Activity
_____
_____
_____

Bird Species/Markings/Features
_____
_____
_____

Notes

Season: _____

Date: _____ Time: _____

Location: _____

Weather/Elements
_____
_____
_____
_____

Place/Location/Habitat
_____
_____
_____
_____

Sights/Sounds & Activity
_____
_____
_____

Bird Species/Markings/Features
_____
_____
_____

Notes

Season: _____

Date: _____ Time: _____

Location: _____

Weather/Elements
_____
_____
_____
_____

Place/Location/Habitat
_____
_____
_____
_____

Sights/Sounds & Activity
_____
_____
_____

Bird Species/Markings/Features
_____
_____
_____

Notes

Season: _____

Date: _____ Time: _____

Location: _____

Weather/Elements
_____
_____
_____
_____

Place/Location/Habitat
_____
_____
_____
_____

Sights/Sounds & Activity
_____
_____
_____

Bird Species/Markings/Features
_____
_____
_____

Notes

Season: _____

Date: _____ Time: _____

Location: _____

Weather/Elements

_____
_____
_____
_____

Place/Location/Habitat

_____
_____
_____
_____

Sights/Sounds & Activity

_____
_____
_____

Bird Species/Markings/Features

_____
_____
_____

Notes

Season: _____

Date: _____ Time: _____

Location: _____

Weather/Elements
_____
_____
_____
_____

Place/Location/Habitat
_____
_____
_____
_____

Sights/Sounds & Activity
_____
_____
_____

Bird Species/Markings/Features
_____
_____
_____

Notes

Season: _____

Date: _____ Time: _____

Location: _____

Weather/Elements
_____
_____
_____
_____

Place/Location/Habitat
_____
_____
_____
_____

Sights/Sounds & Activity
_____
_____
_____

Bird Species/Markings/Features
_____
_____
_____

Notes

Season: _____

Date: _____ Time: _____

Location: _____

Weather/Elements
_____
_____
_____
_____

Place/Location/Habitat
_____
_____
_____
_____

Sights/Sounds & Activity
_____
_____
_____

Bird Species/Markings/Features
_____
_____
_____

Notes

Season: _____

Date: _____ Time: _____

Location: _____

Weather/Elements
_____
_____
_____
_____

Place/Location/Habitat
_____
_____
_____
_____

Sights/Sounds & Activity
_____
_____
_____

Bird Species/Markings/Features
_____
_____
_____

Notes

Season: _____

Date: _____ Time: _____

Location: _____

Weather/Elements
_____
_____
_____
_____

Place/Location/Habitat
_____
_____
_____
_____

Sights/Sounds & Activity
_____
_____
_____

Bird Species/Markings/Features
_____
_____
_____

Notes

Season: _____

Date: _____ Time: _____

Location: _____

Weather/Elements
_____
_____
_____
_____

Place/Location/Habitat
_____
_____
_____
_____

Sights/Sounds & Activity
_____
_____
_____

Bird Species/Markings/Features
_____
_____
_____

Notes

Season: _____

Date: _____ Time: _____

Location: _____

Weather/Elements

_____
_____
_____
_____

Place/Location/Habitat

_____
_____
_____
_____

Sights/Sounds & Activity

_____
_____
_____

Bird Species/Markings/Features

_____
_____
_____

Notes

Season: _____

Date: _____ Time: _____

Location: _____

Weather/Elements
_____
_____
_____
_____

Place/Location/Habitat
_____
_____
_____
_____

Sights/Sounds & Activity
_____
_____
_____

Bird Species/Markings/Features
_____
_____
_____

Notes

Season: _____

Date: _____ Time: _____

Location: _____

Weather/Elements
_____
_____
_____
_____

Place/Location/Habitat
_____
_____
_____
_____

Sights/Sounds & Activity
_____
_____
_____

Bird Species/Markings/Features
_____
_____
_____

Notes

Season: _____

Date: _____ Time: _____

Location: _____

Weather/Elements
_____
_____
_____
_____

Place/Location/Habitat
_____
_____
_____
_____

Sights/Sounds & Activity
_____
_____
_____

Bird Species/Markings/Features
_____
_____
_____

Notes

Season: _____

Date: _____ Time: _____

Location: _____

Weather/Elements
_____
_____
_____
_____

Place/Location/Habitat
_____
_____
_____
_____

Sights/Sounds & Activity
_____
_____
_____

Bird Species/Markings/Features
_____
_____
_____

Notes

Season: _____

Date: _____ Time: _____

Location: _____

Weather/Elements
_____
_____
_____
_____

Place/Location/Habitat
_____
_____
_____
_____

Sights/Sounds & Activity
_____
_____
_____

Bird Species/Markings/Features
_____
_____
_____

Notes

Season: _____

Date: _____ Time: _____

Location: _____

Weather/Elements

_____
_____
_____
_____

Place/Location/Habitat

_____
_____
_____
_____

Sights/Sounds & Activity

_____
_____
_____

Bird Species/Markings/Features

_____
_____
_____

Notes

Season: _____

Date: _____ Time: _____

Location: _____

Weather/Elements

_____
_____
_____
_____

Place/Location/Habitat

_____
_____
_____
_____

Sights/Sounds & Activity

_____
_____
_____

Bird Species/Markings/Features

_____
_____
_____

Notes

Season: _____

Date: _____ Time: _____

Location: _____

Weather/Elements

_____
_____
_____
_____

Place/Location/Habitat

_____
_____
_____
_____

Sights/Sounds & Activity

_____
_____
_____

Bird Species/Markings/Features

_____
_____
_____

Notes

Season: _____

Date: _____ Time: _____

Location: _____

Weather/Elements

_____
_____
_____
_____

Place/Location/Habitat

_____
_____
_____
_____

Sights/Sounds & Activity

_____
_____
_____

Bird Species/Markings/Features

_____
_____
_____

Notes

Season: _____

Date: _____ Time: _____

Location: _____

Weather/Elements
_____
_____
_____
_____

Place/Location/Habitat
_____
_____
_____
_____

Sights/Sounds & Activity
_____
_____
_____

Bird Species/Markings/Features
_____
_____
_____

Notes

Season: _____

Date: _____ Time: _____

Location: _____

Weather/Elements
_____
_____
_____
_____

Place/Location/Habitat
_____
_____
_____
_____

Sights/Sounds & Activity
_____
_____
_____

Bird Species/Markings/Features
_____
_____
_____

Notes

Season: _____

Date: _____ Time: _____

Location: _____

Weather/Elements
_____
_____
_____
_____

Place/Location/Habitat
_____
_____
_____
_____

Sights/Sounds & Activity
_____
_____
_____

Bird Species/Markings/Features
_____
_____
_____

Notes

Season: _____

Date: _____ Time: _____

Location: _____

Weather/Elements
_____
_____
_____
_____

Place/Location/Habitat
_____
_____
_____
_____

Sights/Sounds & Activity
_____
_____
_____

Bird Species/Markings/Features
_____
_____
_____

Notes

Season: _____

Date: _____ Time: _____

Location: _____

Weather/Elements

_____
_____
_____
_____

Place/Location/Habitat

_____
_____
_____
_____

Sights/Sounds & Activity

_____
_____
_____

Bird Species/Markings/Features

_____
_____
_____

Notes

Season: _____

Date: _____ Time: _____

Location: _____

Weather/Elements
_____
_____
_____
_____

Place/Location/Habitat
_____
_____
_____
_____

Sights/Sounds & Activity
_____
_____
_____

Bird Species/Markings/Features
_____
_____
_____

Notes

Season: _____

Date: _____ Time: _____

Location: _____

Weather/Elements
_____
_____
_____
_____

Place/Location/Habitat
_____
_____
_____
_____

Sights/Sounds & Activity
_____
_____
_____

Bird Species/Markings/Features
_____
_____
_____

Notes

Season: _____

Date: _____ Time: _____

Location: _____

Weather/Elements
_____
_____
_____
_____

Place/Location/Habitat
_____
_____
_____
_____

Sights/Sounds & Activity
_____
_____
_____

Bird Species/Markings/Features
_____
_____
_____

Notes

Season: _____

Date: _____ Time: _____

Location: _____

Weather/Elements
_____
_____
_____
_____

Place/Location/Habitat
_____
_____
_____
_____

Sights/Sounds & Activity
_____
_____
_____

Bird Species/Markings/Features
_____
_____
_____

Notes

Season: _____

Date: _____ Time: _____

Location: _____

Weather/Elements

_____
_____
_____
_____

Place/Location/Habitat

_____
_____
_____
_____

Sights/Sounds & Activity

_____
_____
_____

Bird Species/Markings/Features

_____
_____
_____

Notes

Season: _____

Date: _____ Time: _____

Location: _____

Weather/Elements
_____
_____
_____
_____

Place/Location/Habitat
_____
_____
_____
_____

Sights/Sounds & Activity
_____
_____
_____

Bird Species/Markings/Features
_____
_____
_____

Notes

Season: _____

Date: _____ Time: _____

Location: _____

Weather/Elements
_____
_____
_____
_____

Place/Location/Habitat
_____
_____
_____
_____

Sights/Sounds & Activity
_____
_____
_____

Bird Species/Markings/Features
_____
_____
_____

Notes

Season: _____

Date: _____ Time: _____

Location: _____

Weather/Elements
_____
_____
_____
_____

Place/Location/Habitat
_____
_____
_____
_____

Sights/Sounds & Activity
_____
_____
_____

Bird Species/Markings/Features
_____
_____
_____

Notes

Season: _____

Date: _____ Time: _____

Location: _____

Weather/Elements

_____
_____
_____
_____

Place/Location/Habitat

_____
_____
_____
_____

Sights/Sounds & Activity

_____
_____
_____

Bird Species/Markings/Features

_____
_____
_____

Notes

Season: _____

Date: _____ Time: _____

Location: _____

Weather/Elements
_____
_____
_____
_____

Place/Location/Habitat
_____
_____
_____
_____

Sights/Sounds & Activity
_____
_____
_____

Bird Species/Markings/Features
_____
_____
_____

Notes

Season: _____

Date: _____ Time: _____

Location: _____

Weather/Elements
_____
_____
_____
_____

Place/Location/Habitat
_____
_____
_____
_____

Sights/Sounds & Activity
_____
_____
_____

Bird Species/Markings/Features
_____
_____
_____

Notes

Season: _____

Date: _____ Time: _____

Location: _____

Weather/Elements

_____
_____
_____
_____

Place/Location/Habitat

_____
_____
_____
_____

Sights/Sounds & Activity

_____
_____
_____

Bird Species/Markings/Features

_____
_____
_____

Notes

Season: _____

Date: _____ Time: _____

Location: _____

Weather/Elements
_____
_____
_____
_____

Place/Location/Habitat
_____
_____
_____
_____

Sights/Sounds & Activity
_____
_____
_____

Bird Species/Markings/Features
_____
_____
_____

Notes

Season: _____

Date: _____ Time: _____

Location: _____

Weather/Elements
_____
_____
_____
_____

Place/Location/Habitat
_____
_____
_____
_____

Sights/Sounds & Activity
_____
_____
_____

Bird Species/Markings/Features
_____
_____
_____

Notes

Season: _____

Date: _____ Time: _____

Location: _____

Weather/Elements
_____
_____
_____
_____

Place/Location/Habitat
_____
_____
_____
_____

Sights/Sounds & Activity
_____
_____
_____

Bird Species/Markings/Features
_____
_____
_____

Notes

Season: _____

Date: _____ Time: _____

Location: _____

Weather/Elements

_____
_____
_____
_____

Place/Location/Habitat

_____
_____
_____
_____

Sights/Sounds & Activity

_____
_____
_____

Bird Species/Markings/Features

_____
_____
_____

Notes

Season: _____

Date: _____ Time: _____

Location: _____

Weather/Elements
_____
_____
_____
_____

Place/Location/Habitat
_____
_____
_____
_____

Sights/Sounds & Activity
_____
_____
_____

Bird Species/Markings/Features
_____
_____
_____

Notes

Season: _____

Date: _____ Time: _____

Location: _____

Weather/Elements

_____
_____
_____
_____

Place/Location/Habitat

_____
_____
_____
_____

Sights/Sounds & Activity

_____
_____
_____

Bird Species/Markings/Features

_____
_____
_____

Notes

Season: _____

Date: _____ Time: _____

Location: _____

Weather/Elements
_____
_____
_____
_____

Place/Location/Habitat
_____
_____
_____
_____

Sights/Sounds & Activity
_____
_____
_____

Bird Species/Markings/Features
_____
_____
_____

Notes

Season: _____

Date: _____ Time: _____

Location: _____

Weather/Elements
_____
_____
_____
_____

Place/Location/Habitat
_____
_____
_____
_____

Sights/Sounds & Activity
_____
_____
_____

Bird Species/Markings/Features
_____
_____
_____

Notes

Season: _____

Date: _____ Time: _____

Location: _____

Weather/Elements

_____
_____
_____
_____

Place/Location/Habitat

_____
_____
_____
_____

Sights/Sounds & Activity

_____
_____
_____

Bird Species/Markings/Features

_____
_____
_____

Notes

Season: _____

Date: _____ Time: _____

Location: _____

Weather/Elements

_____
_____
_____
_____

Place/Location/Habitat

_____
_____
_____
_____
_____

Sights/Sounds & Activity

_____
_____
_____

Bird Species/Markings/Features

_____
_____
_____

Notes

Season: _____

Date: _____ Time: _____

Location: _____

Weather/Elements
_____
_____
_____
_____

Place/Location/Habitat
_____
_____
_____
_____

Sights/Sounds & Activity
_____
_____
_____

Bird Species/Markings/Features
_____
_____
_____

Notes

Season: _____

Date: _____ Time: _____

Location: _____

Weather/Elements
_____
_____
_____
_____

Place/Location/Habitat
_____
_____
_____
_____

Sights/Sounds & Activity
_____
_____
_____

Bird Species/Markings/Features
_____
_____
_____

Notes

Season: _____

Date: _____ Time: _____

Location: _____

Weather/Elements
_____
_____
_____
_____

Place/Location/Habitat
_____
_____
_____
_____

Sights/Sounds & Activity
_____
_____
_____

Bird Species/Markings/Features
_____
_____
_____

Notes

Season: _____

Date: _____ Time: _____

Location: _____

Weather/Elements

_____
_____
_____
_____

Place/Location/Habitat

_____
_____
_____
_____

Sights/Sounds & Activity

_____
_____
_____

Bird Species/Markings/Features

_____
_____
_____

Notes

Season: _____

Date: _____ Time: _____

Location: _____

Weather/Elements
_____
_____
_____
_____

Place/Location/Habitat
_____
_____
_____
_____

Sights/Sounds & Activity
_____
_____
_____

Bird Species/Markings/Features
_____
_____
_____

Notes

Season: _____

Date: _____ Time: _____

Location: _____

Weather/Elements
_____
_____
_____
_____

Place/Location/Habitat
_____
_____
_____
_____

Sights/Sounds & Activity
_____
_____
_____

Bird Species/Markings/Features
_____
_____
_____

Notes

Season: _____

Date: _____ Time: _____

Location: _____

Weather/Elements
_____
_____
_____
_____

Place/Location/Habitat
_____
_____
_____
_____

Sights/Sounds & Activity
_____
_____
_____

Bird Species/Markings/Features
_____
_____
_____

Notes

Season: _____

Date: _____ Time: _____

Location: _____

Weather/Elements
_____
_____
_____
_____

Place/Location/Habitat
_____
_____
_____
_____

Sights/Sounds & Activity

_____
_____
_____

Bird Species/Markings/Features

_____
_____
_____

Notes

Season: _____

Date: _____ Time: _____

Location: _____

Weather/Elements
_____
_____
_____
_____

Place/Location/Habitat
_____
_____
_____
_____

Sights/Sounds & Activity
_____
_____
_____

Bird Species/Markings/Features
_____
_____
_____

Notes

Season: _____

Date: _____ Time: _____

Location: _____

Weather/Elements

_____
_____
_____
_____

Place/Location/Habitat

_____
_____
_____
_____

Sights/Sounds & Activity

_____
_____
_____

Bird Species/Markings/Features

_____
_____
_____

Notes

Season: _____

Date: _____ Time: _____

Location: _____

Weather/Elements
_____
_____
_____
_____

Place/Location/Habitat
_____
_____
_____
_____

Sights/Sounds & Activity
_____
_____
_____

Bird Species/Markings/Features
_____
_____
_____

Notes

Season: _____

Date: _____ Time: _____

Location: _____

Weather/Elements
_____
_____
_____
_____

Place/Location/Habitat
_____
_____
_____
_____

Sights/Sounds & Activity
_____
_____
_____

Bird Species/Markings/Features
_____
_____
_____

Notes

Season: _____

Date: _____ Time: _____

Location: _____

Weather/Elements
_____
_____
_____
_____

Place/Location/Habitat
_____
_____
_____
_____

Sights/Sounds & Activity
_____
_____
_____

Bird Species/Markings/Features
_____
_____
_____

Notes

Season: _____

Date: _____ Time: _____

Location: _____

Weather/Elements
_____
_____
_____
_____

Place/Location/Habitat
_____
_____
_____
_____

Sights/Sounds & Activity
_____
_____
_____

Bird Species/Markings/Features
_____
_____
_____

Notes

Season: _____

Date: _____ Time: _____

Location: _____

Weather/Elements

_____
_____
_____
_____

Place/Location/Habitat

_____
_____
_____
_____

Sights/Sounds & Activity

_____
_____
_____

Bird Species/Markings/Features

_____
_____
_____

Notes

Season: _____

Date: _____ Time: _____

Location: _____

Weather/Elements
_____
_____
_____
_____

Place/Location/Habitat
_____
_____
_____
_____

Sights/Sounds & Activity

_____
_____
_____

Bird Species/Markings/Features

_____
_____
_____

Notes

Season: _____

Date: _____ Time: _____

Location: _____

Weather/Elements
_____
_____
_____
_____

Place/Location/Habitat
_____
_____
_____
_____

Sights/Sounds & Activity
_____
_____
_____

Bird Species/Markings/Features
_____
_____
_____

Notes

Season: _____

Date: _____ Time: _____

Location: _____

Weather/Elements
_____
_____
_____
_____

Place/Location/Habitat
_____
_____
_____
_____

Sights/Sounds & Activity
_____
_____
_____

Bird Species/Markings/Features
_____
_____
_____

Notes

Season: _____

Date: _____ Time: _____

Location: _____

Weather/Elements
_____
_____
_____
_____

Place/Location/Habitat
_____
_____
_____
_____

Sights/Sounds & Activity
_____
_____
_____

Bird Species/Markings/Features
_____
_____
_____

Notes

Season: _____

Date: _____ Time: _____

Location: _____

Weather/Elements
_____
_____
_____
_____

Place/Location/Habitat
_____
_____
_____
_____

Sights/Sounds & Activity
_____
_____
_____

Bird Species/Markings/Features
_____
_____
_____

Notes

Season: _____

Date: _____ Time: _____

Location: _____

Weather/Elements

_____
_____
_____
_____

Place/Location/Habitat

_____
_____
_____
_____

Sights/Sounds & Activity

_____
_____
_____

Bird Species/Markings/Features

_____
_____
_____

Notes

Season: _____

Date: _____ Time: _____

Location: _____

Weather/Elements

_____
_____
_____
_____

Place/Location/Habitat

_____
_____
_____
_____

Sights/Sounds & Activity

_____
_____
_____

Bird Species/Markings/Features

_____
_____
_____

Notes

Season: _____

Date: _____ Time: _____

Location: _____

Weather/Elements
_____
_____
_____
_____

Place/Location/Habitat
_____
_____
_____
_____

Sights/Sounds & Activity
_____
_____
_____

Bird Species/Markings/Features
_____
_____
_____

Notes

Season: _____

Date: _____ Time: _____

Location: _____

Weather/Elements
_____
_____
_____
_____

Place/Location/Habitat
_____
_____
_____
_____

Sights/Sounds & Activity
_____
_____
_____

Bird Species/Markings/Features
_____
_____
_____

Notes

Season: _____

Date: _____ Time: _____

Location: _____

Weather/Elements

_____
_____
_____
_____

Place/Location/Habitat

_____
_____
_____
_____

Sights/Sounds & Activity

_____
_____
_____

Bird Species/Markings/Features

_____
_____
_____

Notes

Season: _____

Date: _____ Time: _____

Location: _____

Weather/Elements

_____
_____
_____
_____

Place/Location/Habitat

_____
_____
_____
_____

Sights/Sounds & Activity

_____
_____
_____

Bird Species/Markings/Features

_____
_____
_____

Notes

Season: _____

Date: _____ Time: _____

Location: _____

Weather/Elements

_____
_____
_____
_____

Place/Location/Habitat

_____
_____
_____
_____

Sights/Sounds & Activity

_____
_____
_____

Bird Species/Markings/Features

_____
_____
_____

Notes

Season: _____

Date: _____ Time: _____

Location: _____

Weather/Elements
_____
_____
_____
_____

Place/Location/Habitat
_____
_____
_____
_____

Sights/Sounds & Activity
_____
_____
_____

Bird Species/Markings/Features
_____
_____
_____

Notes

Season: _____

Date: _____ Time: _____

Location: _____

Weather/Elements
_____
_____
_____
_____

Place/Location/Habitat
_____
_____
_____
_____

Sights/Sounds & Activity
_____
_____
_____

Bird Species/Markings/Features
_____
_____
_____

Notes

Season: _____

Date: _____ Time: _____

Location: _____

Weather/Elements
_____
_____
_____
_____

Place/Location/Habitat
_____
_____
_____
_____

Sights/Sounds & Activity
_____
_____

Bird Species/Markings/Features
_____
_____

Notes

Season: _____

Date: _____ Time: _____

Location: _____

Weather/Elements
_____
_____
_____
_____

Place/Location/Habitat
_____
_____
_____
_____

Sights/Sounds & Activity
_____
_____
_____

Bird Species/Markings/Features
_____
_____
_____

Notes

Season: _____

Date: _____ Time: _____

Location: _____

Weather/Elements

_____
_____
_____
_____

Place/Location/Habitat

_____
_____
_____
_____

Sights/Sounds & Activity

_____
_____
_____

Bird Species/Markings/Features

_____
_____
_____

Notes

Season: _____

Date: _____ Time: _____

Location: _____

Weather/Elements
_____
_____
_____
_____

Place/Location/Habitat
_____
_____
_____
_____

Sights/Sounds & Activity
_____
_____
_____

Bird Species/Markings/Features
_____
_____
_____

Notes

Season: _____

Date: _____ Time: _____

Location: _____

Weather/Elements
_____
_____
_____
_____

Place/Location/Habitat
_____
_____
_____
_____

Sights/Sounds & Activity
_____
_____
_____

Bird Species/Markings/Features
_____
_____
_____

Notes

Season: _____

Date: _____ Time: _____

Location: _____

Weather/Elements
_____
_____
_____
_____

Place/Location/Habitat
_____
_____
_____
_____

Sights/Sounds & Activity
_____
_____
_____

Bird Species/Markings/Features
_____
_____
_____

Notes

Season: _____

Date: _____ Time: _____

Location: _____

Weather/Elements

_____
_____
_____
_____

Place/Location/Habitat

_____
_____
_____
_____

Sights/Sounds & Activity

_____
_____
_____

Bird Species/Markings/Features

_____
_____
_____

Notes

Season: _____

Date: _____ Time: _____

Location: _____

Weather/Elements
_____
_____
_____
_____

Place/Location/Habitat
_____
_____
_____
_____

Sights/Sounds & Activity
_____
_____
_____

Bird Species/Markings/Features
_____
_____
_____

Notes

Season: _____

Date: _____ Time: _____

Location: _____

Weather/Elements

_____
_____
_____
_____

Place/Location/Habitat

_____
_____
_____
_____

Sights/Sounds & Activity

_____
_____
_____

Bird Species/Markings/Features

_____
_____
_____

Notes

Season: _____

Date: _____ Time: _____

Location: _____

Weather/Elements
_____
_____
_____
_____

Place/Location/Habitat
_____
_____
_____
_____

Sights/Sounds & Activity
_____
_____
_____

Bird Species/Markings/Features
_____
_____
_____

Notes

Season: _____

Date: _____ Time: _____

Location: _____

Weather/Elements
_____
_____
_____
_____

Place/Location/Habitat
_____
_____
_____
_____

Sights/Sounds & Activity
_____
_____
_____

Bird Species/Markings/Features
_____
_____
_____

Notes

Season: _____

Date: _____ Time: _____

Location: _____

Weather/Elements
_____
_____
_____
_____

Place/Location/Habitat
_____
_____
_____
_____

Sights/Sounds & Activity
_____
_____
_____

Bird Species/Markings/Features
_____
_____
_____

Notes

Season: _____

Date: _____ Time: _____

Location: _____

Weather/Elements
_____
_____
_____
_____

Place/Location/Habitat
_____
_____
_____
_____

Sights/Sounds & Activity
_____
_____
_____

Bird Species/Markings/Features
_____
_____
_____

Notes

Season: _____

Date: _____ Time: _____

Location: _____

Weather/Elements
_____
_____
_____
_____

Place/Location/Habitat
_____
_____
_____
_____

Sights/Sounds & Activity
_____
_____
_____

Bird Species/Markings/Features
_____
_____
_____

Notes

Season: _____

Date: _____ Time: _____

Location: _____

Weather/Elements
_____
_____
_____
_____

Place/Location/Habitat
_____
_____
_____
_____

Sights/Sounds & Activity
_____
_____
_____

Bird Species/Markings/Features
_____
_____
_____

Notes

Season: _____

Date: _____ Time: _____

Location: _____

Weather/Elements
_____
_____
_____
_____

Place/Location/Habitat
_____
_____
_____
_____

Sights/Sounds & Activity
_____
_____
_____

Bird Species/Markings/Features
_____
_____
_____

Notes

Season: _____

Date: _____ Time: _____

Location: _____

Weather/Elements
_____
_____
_____
_____

Place/Location/Habitat
_____
_____
_____
_____

Sights/Sounds & Activity
_____
_____
_____

Bird Species/Markings/Features
_____
_____
_____

Notes

Season: _____

Date: _____ Time: _____

Location: _____

Weather/Elements
_____
_____
_____
_____

Place/Location/Habitat
_____
_____
_____
_____

Sights/Sounds & Activity
_____
_____
_____

Bird Species/Markings/Features
_____
_____
_____

Notes

Season: _____

Date: _____ Time: _____

Location: _____

Weather/Elements
_____
_____
_____
_____

Place/Location/Habitat
_____
_____
_____
_____

Sights/Sounds & Activity
_____
_____
_____

Bird Species/Markings/Features
_____
_____
_____

Notes

Season: _____

Date: _____ Time: _____

Location: _____

Weather/Elements
_____
_____
_____
_____

Place/Location/Habitat
_____
_____
_____
_____

Sights/Sounds & Activity
_____
_____
_____

Bird Species/Markings/Features
_____
_____
_____

Notes

Season: _____

Date: _____ Time: _____

Location: _____

Weather/Elements

_____
_____
_____
_____

Place/Location/Habitat

_____
_____
_____
_____

Sights/Sounds & Activity

_____
_____
_____

Bird Species/Markings/Features

_____
_____
_____

Notes

Season: _____

Date: _____ Time: _____

Location: _____

Weather/Elements

_____
_____
_____
_____

Place/Location/Habitat

_____
_____
_____
_____

Sights/Sounds & Activity

_____
_____
_____

Bird Species/Markings/Features

_____
_____
_____

Notes

Season: _____

Date: _____ Time: _____

Location: _____

Weather/Elements
_____
_____
_____
_____

Place/Location/Habitat
_____
_____
_____
_____

Sights/Sounds & Activity
_____
_____
_____

Bird Species/Markings/Features
_____
_____
_____

Notes

Season: _____

Date: _____ Time: _____

Location: _____

Weather/Elements
_____
_____
_____
_____

Place/Location/Habitat
_____
_____
_____
_____

Sights/Sounds & Activity
_____
_____
_____

Bird Species/Markings/Features
_____
_____
_____

Notes

Season: _____

Date: _____ Time: _____

Location: _____

Weather/Elements
_____
_____
_____
_____

Place/Location/Habitat
_____
_____
_____
_____

Sights/Sounds & Activity
_____
_____
_____

Bird Species/Markings/Features
_____
_____
_____

Notes

Season: _____

Date: _____ Time: _____

Location: _____

Weather/Elements

_____
_____
_____
_____

Place/Location/Habitat

_____
_____
_____
_____

Sights/Sounds & Activity

_____
_____
_____

Bird Species/Markings/Features

_____
_____
_____

Notes

Season: _____

Date: _____ Time: _____

Location: _____

Weather/Elements
_____
_____
_____
_____

Place/Location/Habitat
_____
_____
_____
_____

Sights/Sounds & Activity
_____
_____
_____

Bird Species/Markings/Features
_____
_____
_____

Notes

Season: _____

Date: _____ Time: _____

Location: _____

Weather/Elements
_____
_____
_____
_____

Place/Location/Habitat
_____
_____
_____
_____

Sights/Sounds & Activity
_____
_____
_____

Bird Species/Markings/Features
_____
_____
_____

Notes

Manufactured by Amazon.ca
Bolton, ON

13504180R00072